KNOW YOUR CHRISTIANS

Ten Witnesses
for God

D1744539

KNOW YOUR CHRISTIANS

Ten Witnesses
for God

by
WILLIAM PURCELL
Canon Emeritus of Worcester

MOWBRAY
LONDON & OXFORD

First published 1987
by A.R. Mowbray & Co. Ltd,
Saint Thomas House, Becket Street,
Oxford, OX1 1SJ.

Typeset by Comersgate Art Studios Ltd, 52 St Clements Street,
Oxford OX4 1AG.
Printed in Great Britain by Cox and Wyman Ltd., Reading.

British Library Cataloguing in Publication Data
Purcell, William
Ten witnesses for God.—(Know your Christians).
1. Christian biography
I. Title   II. Series
209'.2'2   BR 1700.2

ISBN 0-264-67128-7

CONTENTS

INTRODUCTION

Witnesses of God come in many kinds. They are those who have, either by word or deed, and often by both, made God seem particularly real to all kinds of people in their day and age. They are living evidence of what God has meant to them, and what they believe God should mean for other people.

It is as if there is always a trial going on between those who are against God, either in the sense that they do not believe that he exists, or feeling that he does not matter, and those who believe him to be blazingly real because they have found him blazingly real. That happened, and in the modern cases is still happening, to the ten men featured in this book. George Fox, a Quaker, found him everywhere, William Grimshaw of Haworth found him all around. George Whitefield, who started life as a pot-boy in a Gloucester inn and became one of the greatest preachers of his century, stood up and witnessed for him through the spoken word. So did Charles Spurgeon a hundred years later. So, and in their own particular way, did Sankey and Moody, the American evangelists in the nineteenth century. So still does Billy Graham in our own time.

But there are also those who are powerful witnesses for God by what they do and by what happens to them. David Watson, with his wonderful ministry in St Michael-le-Belfrey in York only a few years ago, spoke to thousands through the witness of his life. Father Popieluszko, although he is now dead, murdered by secret police, is astonishingly real as a true witness for God in modern Poland. And, in Britain, David Sheppard, Bishop of Liverpool, with his emphasis on the needs of the poor in our great cities, gives powerful testimony to the reality of the God who enables him to speak and act with such power.

the scriptures but also to live by them in all respects. All weapons of war were to be put away in favour of the weapon of the armour of the spirit. The quakers were totally incorruptible people, as indeed they still are. Nothing could sway them from their conviction. They were imprisoned, sometimes in large numbers, because of their utter outspokenness. They would not speak respectfully to judges. They would not pay a church-tithe, which in those early days was demanded of all citizens. They would not take an oath in court.

There was one early quaker named James Naylor, in London, who was so carried away by his message that he once staged a dramatic entry into the city of Bristol, riding a donkey and accompanied by followers crying out hosannas in imitation of the triumphant entry of Christ into Jerusalem. For this act, which was seen as blasphemy, he was branded on the forehead with the letter B and whipped through the city at the cart's tail. He also had his tongue bored through and was thrown into prison. Yet, afterwards, he could say: 'there is a spirit which I feel delights to do no evil, nor to revenge any wrong; but delights to endure all things in hope to enjoy its own in the end. Its hope is to outlive all wrath and contention and to weary out all exaltation and cruelty . . . As it bares no evil in itself so it conceives none in thought to any other. If it be betrayed, it bares it, for its ground and spring is the mercies and forgiveness of God, its crown in meakness. . .' Such is still very much the Quaker attitude to the world, and

3

they have continued steadfast in it.

George Fox was born in 1624 at Fenney Drayton, in Leicestershire, the son of a puritan weaver. He became a shoemaker; but at the age of nineteen felt called to give up his family and friends and to go out into the world seeking christian truths, which he found it impossible to come upon in formal religion. Those were days of great debate among the churches in Britain and elsewhere – bodies which, in Fox's view, dealt in secondhand answers. What he wanted was something entirely new, a direct revelation of his salvation through Christ's. In 1646 he achieved this through a reliance on what he called the 'inner light of the living Christ'. In 1647 he began to preach; two years later he was put in prison in Nottingham, then in Derby, then in other places. But nothing would silence or discourage him. His was a painful searching after truth, and it was his ultimate certainty that he found it. Swarthmore Hall, in the Lake District, became his headquarters, and is still in possession of the Society of Friends. It had been the home of Thomas Fell, Vice-Chancellor of the Duchy of Lancaster, whose widow, Margaret, George Fox married. From this base he began his missionary journeys to Ireland, to the West Indies, to Holland. His followers crossed the Atlantic, sometimes with dire results.

The puritans of New England were offended by the quakers, to take one notable and tragic instance, when they came among them and condemned them for being so exclusive. But these puritans had left their homes in England precisely in order to be exclusive and to set up in New England a christian community based upon their own hard-won convictions of truth and justice and righteousness. When the quakers questioned this they were banished; few obeyed, and as a result three were hanged on Boston Common, choosing, in the characteristic quaker manner, to stick by their convictions rather than obey authority. But they died in a good cause: so great was the indignation against the executions that a greater sense of tolerance came upon the scene and the principles of religious liberty were strengthened.

But there were also noble results from the quaker influence in America, as there were in Britain. The same James Naylor, who had been whipped at the cart's tail in Bristol for blasphemy, visited the American Indians. Quite fearlessly, he urged them to turn from darkness to light, to accept Christ in their own hearts, and to follow him henceforward. Strangely, among the wild people, he was well received: he lived in a wigwam as their guest and began a relationship of mutual trust with a people whom few others had ever been able to get alongside. Today, as a direct result of this early example of mutual trust, many once-primitive peoples have been attracted to quakerism.

Another very famous quaker who lived according to this pattern was William Penn, founder of Pennsylvania. Here was a distinguished man who had been greatly affected by a quaker tradesman he had heard preaching in Cork in 1665. He was moved to become a quaker himself and was imprisoned for it but later acquitted in a famous trial. He became interested in the foundation of a colony in America which would make possible liberty of conscience for quakers and others. Thus Pennsylvania emerged, first as a colony, and later as a state of the union. William Penn was able to live in peace with the Indian tribes just as James Naylor had some years before him.

The followers of George Fox could not only be disturbing, therefore, they also had their own quiet manner of dealing with difficult moral situations which was very effective. There was a man called John Woolman, a tailor in New Jersey, America, who, in later years, could not accept the institution of slavery, being convinced that it was wrong. This was almost a century after the days of Naylor and William Penn but the manner remained. If Woolman happened to be staying in a home where a slave served at table he would insist on paying for the services rendered. Nothing could shake him. It was a non-aggressive protest of great effectiveness, a kind of non-violent revolution which, down the years, members of the Society of Friends have shown, surprisingly often, to be a decisive influence on events.

But the story of the quakers always comes back to George Fox. He wrote a detailed account of his experiences in his famous *Journal*, and it is from this that we can gather something of his message, and also get a vivid impression of the manner in which he wrote and spoke. From his earliest preaching and travelling days in England, for instance, there is this account of one of the many occasions when he was put in prison: 'Then, passing from thence, I heard of a people in prison in Coventry for religion. As I walked towards the gaol, the word of the Lord came to me saying, "my love was always to thee, and thou art in my love". And I was ravished with the sense of the love of God, and greatly strengthened in my inward man. But when I came into the gaol where those prisoners were, a great power of darkness struck at me; and I sat still, having my spirit gathered into the love of God.' It is easy to see, in the mind's eye, a group of humble people, men and women, held together in the stench and the darkness of that primitive prison in Coventry, for the crime of preaching the truth about Christ as they saw it. Down the years many quakers have suffered for their convictions, many of them as conscientious objectors in war-time. They have always been, to some extent, marked with that exclusiveness which some of the early quakers found blameworthy in the Puritans of New England. But they have always been just, and kind, and generous, and, though their faith has sometimes seemed to be for the few, quakers have always reached out to the many – as they still do – in love and charity. Yet George Fox's way has never been an easy one to follow because he required very high standards, not only in others, but particularly in himself. He summed it all up in a passage in his *Journal*: 'One day, when I had been walking solitarily abroad, and was come home, I was taken up in the love of God, so that I could not but admire the greatness of his love; and while I was in that condition, it was opened unto me by the eternal light and power, and I therein clearly saw. That all that was done and to be done in and by Christ, and how he conquers and destroys this tempt to the devil, and all his works, and is atop of him; and that all these troubles were good for me, and temptations for the trial of my faith, which Christ had given me. My living faith was raised, that I saw all was done by Christ the life, and my belief was in him. When at anytime my condition was veiled, my secret belief was stayed firm, and hope underneath held me, as an anchor in the bottom of the sea, and anchored my immortal soul. . .'

His was a magnetic personality and he had great spiritual power. He also had a totally selfless devotion and patience in persecution, as his record shows. He died on 13 January 1691. The Society of Friends, world-wide, is his living memorial.

WILLIAM GRIMSHAW

(1708–63)

The Man on the Moors

People in the wild moorland township of Haworth, high in the hills of West Yorkshire where the shaggy country reaches over the Pennines into Lancashire, knew that a very unusual person had come among them when, in the year 1742, a man called William Grimshaw appeared on the scene. He could scarcely have come to a tougher place. The natives of Haworth, later to be famous as the birthplace of the Brontë sisters, were renowned for their extreme roughness amounting almost to savagery, especially towards strangers. Few visitors, as a general rule, made their way up the valley from the nearest town, Keighley, which was down in the valley towards Bradford. The township itself, at the top of a steep hill, gave straight onto the moors which stretched, wild and forbidding, in all directions, where the wind moaned through the heather and ruffled the wool of the sheep, the only living creatures common to the place. So Haworth was self-enclosed and ready to look with immediate suspicion upon any newcomer.

But in the newcomer, William Grimshaw, who had come among them as perpetual curate, (the odd title given to clergymen who were sent to a parish by licence from their bishop without any formal institution) they found something special. Grimshaw was not a man to be moved easily, nor shifted in the slightest degree from what he saw as his duty. And in Haworth he was to have a most remarkable ministry, ended only by his death twenty-one years later from a fever caught while visiting a sick parishioner. But during those twenty-one years many dramatic things happened, and William Grimshaw made his mark upon the place and upon his times in a way that has endured.

He was a very big man, which was a help when it came to dealing with some of the rougher ways of his parishioners. But even before he came to Haworth his life had been a fairly rugged one. He was born in Lancashire where he went to Blackburn Grammar School and from there to Christ's College, Cambridge. Ordained deacon in 1731, he became a curate first at Rochdale, then at Todmorden on the other side of the Pennines from Haworth. Those were not good times for the Church or the christian faith. Indifference was everywhere and there was brutality in much of society, especially among the poor. During those middle years of the eighteenth century it seemed to many people as though God had died or had never even existed, or was at any rate a power no longer of any influence or interest. In many cases, though by no means in all, this outlook was reflected in the attitudes of some clergy to their duties, so that the indifferent or careless parson could quite easily be found in the towns and villages of England. Grimshaw himself, in his early years in orders, mirrored this mood. He lived a careless life, even a dissolute one, for some time. But it was the sudden death of his wife, whom he had dearly loved, which proved a turning point for him.

His wife's death led to a period of intense spiritual struggle in Grimshaw, in which he strove to find some centre of belief, some living God. Strangely, he did not seem to know that men like George Whitefield, John Wesley and other early evangelicals were at work, spreading the gospel and awakening in many a new life of faith and hope. At any rate, none of them came his way. But what did, were the writings of some of the puritan thinkers of his time. These, with their insistence upon the reality of God and the need to find and serve him, profoundly affected Grimshaw. He became a changed man, and it was as such that he went up to the moors at Haworth in 1742.

Now at last Grimshaw made contact with some of the early evangelicals who, with their preaching of the gospel, were arousing people all over the land. The time was to come when he was to meet Wesley, Whitefield, and the famous Henry Venn, Vicar of Huddersfield during some of the years when Grimshaw was up at Haworth, and whose piety and zeal made a great impression. But, for the moment, Grimshaw's first duty was to clean up, and then to arouse with the gospel, his own parish. No true idea of the greatness of his achievement there is possible without remembering always the brutal nature of most of the people; but soon Grimshaw's influence began to be felt.

Some strange reports came out of Haworth. One was that on Sunday mornings it was inadvisable to be caught by the parson drinking in the pub, which stood, as it still does, next-door to the church. The rumours were that, if men in the bar saw him approaching, armed as usual with a whip, they would scramble through the windows and make off as fast as they could go, knowing that if he caught them the parson would whip them into church. Grimshaw enforced the keeping of Sunday in all kinds of ways, including this one. He also stopped Haworth Races, which were frequently the scene of brutal disorders. So before very long he became formidable and feared. But he also became much loved, which was the other side of the coin, and this, more than any of the ferocious discipline which he was able to enforce because of the power of his personality, gave him his real strength. Everyone respected him; some came to love him dearly. The number of people going to the communion in Haworth Church when he arrived was, on average, twelve. Within three years it was twelve hundred. What is more, people in trouble, people in sickness, the poor and the forgotten knew that in him they had a friend. For from him came what they could not feel to be the true love of Christ, reaching out to them.

Before very long the scene of Grimshaw's activities widened dramatically, not only into the parishes around, over the moors into Lancashire, down the valley towards Keighley and Bradford, but also into the country as a whole. Part of the reason for this, in addition to his own increasing fame, was his friendship with the Wesleys, with Whitefield, and with those other evangelicals whom he had now discovered. They themselves were much attracted to him and John Wesley, in particular, had a profound admiration for Grimshaw. He even suggested in later years that Grimshaw should succeed him in his leading role over the developing methodist body in Britain. People would come from far and near to hear Grimshaw preach; but soon they were coming across the hills and up into the moors to hear some of these famous men whom Grimshaw had invited to his pulpit. So it came to pass that, in the remote church in Haworth, most of the leading figures of the religious revival of the day came, from time to time, to preach, including such extraordinary figures as John Nelson, a stonemason, who was one of Wesley's most celebrated lay preachers. Haworth was being woken up.

None of this was universally approved, however. Local clergy, in particular, resented Grimshaw's extraordinary fame and even more extraordinary results. They, among others, pointed out that it was illegal, as was the case in those times, to invite such men as the famous Whitefield to preach in an anglican pulpit. They also felt that it was out of order for Grimshaw himself, as he commonly did, to preach far and wide, far beyond the boundaries of his own parish, where his homely and forceful language had instant appeal. There were times when this opposition took a serious form. There was, for instance, a riot in the town of Colne, Lancashire, where he was mugged by a mob who dragged him down and beat him. This was only one instance of the kind of treatment which Grimshaw had to suffer from time to time. Yet he survived and continued with his enormously powerful witness to the faith.

Grimshaw's own deep and obvious sincerity was a powerful factor influencing those in authority in his favour. Among them was the Archbishop of York, Matthew Hutton, who gave Grimshaw permission to continue, and who did much by his authority to counter the charges of those who maintained that Grimshaw was breaking the law by his irregular activities.

By the time Grimshaw made the sick visit which led to his death, his fame had spread widely. No longer was Haworth a wild place up in the moors, unvisited and virtually unknown. Famous men came to its church, all kinds of men and women made their way to hear them. And the people of the place itself, no longer as fierce and rough as once they were, had come to a great admiration for their parson and, in very many cases, to a real love for him. But not quite everything went well for Grimshaw. He had a daughter who died as a child at school which was a shattering blow, needing much of his faith to overcome it. Perhaps an even graver sorrow, if that were possible, was the conduct of his own son who, growing up wild and dissolute, rather like Grimshaw in his own youth, was a source of much anxiety. He was in that state when William Grimshaw died. From then on the son became a changed man, putting behind him his evil ways. Perhaps, after all, this was Grimshaw's truest memorial.

GEORGE WHITEFIELD

(1714–70)

The Enthusiast

He was amazing; he was extraordinary; some said he
was the greatest preacher ever. It was reported that his
first sermon sent fifteen people mad. Many said he was
one of those whom serious folk in the eighteenth
century in England felt were dangerous – 'an enthusiast', meaning someone who had more passion than
sense and whose influence was bad. He was also a very
great man, had a stunning effect in the American
colonies. His preaching tour of New England in the
Autumn of 1740, when he addressed crowds of up to
eight thousand nearly every day for a month, was
probably the most sensational event in the whole
history of American religion. Wherever he went in
those early years – New England, New York, Philadelphia, Charleston, Savannah – he left, it has been said 'a
lively interest in religion'. There were hundreds for
whom the sole important question had become, 'What
must I do to be saved?', and he left not a few who
wondered what awakened religion would do to the
social family. Whitefield was, in short, a phenomenon.

He was born in the Bell Inn in Gloucester, and by
the age of sixteen was a barman in the same place. But

he was always thinking of another career, another calling, something which he could not quite in those early years identify but which he knew was to be his destiny. Eventually he managed to get to Oxford as a servitor at Pembroke College. There he waited at a table on the other undergraduates and received in payment his education. This is where he met the 'Methodists', the group of other men, who included John Wesley, who were then beginning a movement which was to lead to the great revival.

Like the other Oxford methodists, Whitefield's chief concern was to live a quiet and devout holy life. But just before the Easter of 1735 a great thing happened to him: he underwent an experience which he after described as a new birth. He said: 'I was delivered from the burden that had so heavily suppressed me. The spirit of mourning was taken from me, and I knew what it was to truly rejoice in God my saviour.' This sudden conversion had amazing results, releasing a flood of eloquence the like of which has rarely been known in this country and which, during his visits to America, brought something into that land which had never before been experienced there. But first there was a time of preparation.

Whitefield was ordained as an anglican clergyman and was for a time a curate in a Oxfordshire village. Shortly after that he decided to cross the Atlantic to Georgia in America where a certain General Oglethorpe had founded a settlement for men and women from Britain who were aiming at a fresh start in life. So

17

Whitefield started to preach, partly in order to raise money for this project and for his travel. It was about this time that he gave that first sermon in Gloucester after which the bishop of that place said that he had sent fifteen people mad. Thus, very early on, people began to find something very strange and powerful in Whitefield's unique preaching with its dramatic message of salvation. And, equally, some disapproved of it.

Whitefield spoke everywhere. In Bristol, for example, he had heard of the physical and spiritual degradation of the colliers of Kingswood Chase, a few miles outside, who were so tough that they were left severely alone by everybody else. Whitefield decided that he would persuade them that God at least cared for them. This was the origin of the famous phrase, later taken up by John Wesley, 'Go not to those who want you, but to those who want you most.' The effect of his preaching on these rough and simple people was incredible and they were soon experiencing conversion in crowds. Nor was that all: Whitefield decided to try and build a school for the children of the colliers and to help the men and women themselves to a more decent sort of life. This was where he made particular contact with John Wesley, whom he asked to go and carry on the work there after he himself had gone to America for the second time.

From 1736 to 1739 Whitefield was ceasely occupied with his preaching and his mission in America. He founded an orphan house which still stands on the road from Brunswick to Savannah. On his return to Britain for a while he went again to Bristol where, because people remembered the power of his first visit, it was said that they, on this second occasion when he was billed to preach, 'hung upon the rails of the orphan loft, others climbed upon the leads of the church, and altogether made the church so hot with their breath that the steam would fall from the pillars like drops of rain.' It was because of the effects of this kind of his preaching that Whitefield, like Wesley, was forbidden the use of churches and began his utterances in the open air.

His style of preaching has often been praised and sometimes, with equal vigour, criticised. But the effects were undoubted. It was said that even the cynical Lord Chesterfield, when Whitefield was telling in his presence of the career of a blind man tottering towards a precipice, suddenly leapt from his chair and shouted: 'By God! He's over!' But, for all this dramatic effect-seeking, Whitefield was completely sincere and a man indeed of noble character. His was by far the most impelling personality of the great revival in Britain and his effect upon John Wesley, and all which happened in the methodist revival afterwards, was profound, even though the two for various reasons fell out in later years.

But what was Whitefield's message? He was convinced that God had from eternity predestined the majority of mankind to damnation, and only a few to salvation through Jesus Christ. So that the purpose of his preaching was to gather to Christ those who were predestined to salvation. It has to be said, however, that so great was his own sense of God's love that he gave the impression that this love would nonetheless be given to all men who turned to God. This doctrine of predestination, as it was called, was rejected by the Wesleys totally, and it was the main reason for the separation between them. The Wesleys were quite sure that Christ had really and truly died for all men. They agreed that the first move in any act of salvation was God's; but they refused to draw from this the conclusion that there was no free choice between damnation and salvation.

One person who was herself converted by Whitefield's preaching and who came to be his most notable supporter was Selina, Countess of Huntington. She had been influenced by the methodists of the Holy Club from the beginning, and she persuaded a fair number of her aristocratic friends that methodists were acceptable and they should be heard. Indeed, after a time, she came to select the methodist preachers whom she thought the polite world ought to hear and often built little chapels for them to preach in. This is the origin of the present chapels, still to be found in some English centres, called chapels of 'The Countess of Huntington's Connexion.'

But it was in America, without a doubt, that the greatest impact was made by the former tapster of the Bell Inn. It was in 1739, when he first went there, that he was seen to be a speaker of the American scene whose zeal was so great and whose abilities so powerful that he altered the conventions of preaching forever after. He was twenty-five when he began his amazing career on the other side of the Atlantic. There he evoked a mass religious response of a size which had never before been witnessed in the colonies. Many could understand Whitefield's revival only as a special outpouring of divine grace and came to call it the 'Great Awakening'. Why was Whitefield so amazingly successful?.

One of the men who observed him closely and respected him greatly was none other than Benjamin Franklin, a very notable American thinker and writer who was one of those who helped frame a Declaration of Independence in the United States. That such a man so greatly admired him signified the quality of Whitefield.

Franklin was part of a crowd who attended one of Whitefield's first American preachings in Philadelphia. He noticed the astonishing fact that, for one thing, Whitefield could be heard clearly by a crowd numbering more than twenty thousand at one time. He noted also his tremendous speaking endurance as well as the quality of his diction and the power of his message. Whitefield was certainly tireless. From the time he began preaching at twenty-three years old until his death thirty-three years later, it is said that he preached several times weekly to audiences of this size.

Benjamin Franklin wrote this account of White-field in action: 'He had a loud and clear voice, and articulated his words and sentences so perfectly that he may be heard and understood at a great distance, especially as those who heard him kept the most complete silence. He preached one evening from the top of the Court House steps, which are in the middle of Market Street and on the west side of Second Street. Both streets were filled with his hearers to a considerable distance. Being among the hindermost in Market Street I had the curiosity to learn how far he could be heard by walking back-wards down towards the river. I found his voice distinct.' He then added something typical of his scientific curiosity: 'Imagining a semi-circle of which my distance should be the radius, and that it was filled with auditors each of whom I allowed two square feet, I computed that he might well be heard by more than thirty thousand. This reconciled me to the newspaper accounts of his having preached to twenty-five thousand people in the fields . . . Every accent, every emphasis, every modulation of voice was so perfectly well tuned and well placed that, without being interested in the subject, one could not help being pleased with the discourse, a pleasure of much the same kind as that received from an excellent piece of music.'

Certainly the same kind of opposition came to Whitefield in America as it did in England, and for the same reason – that he was held to be that dangerous thing, an enthusiast. But, as with Jesus himself, 'the common people heard him gladly'. An American colonist called Nathan Cole gave an astonishing account of how the 'common people' would go to enormous lengths just to hear Whitefield and how they were always excited by his message. It was in the October of 1740 that Cole wrote this account: 'Then on a sudden, in the morning at about eight or nine on the clock there came a messenger and said that Mr Whitefield preached at Hartford and is to preach at Middletown this morning at ten on the clock. I was in my field at work. I dropped my tool that I had in my hand and ran home to my wife telling her to make ready quickly and to go and hear Mr Whitefield preach. Then I ran to my pasture for my horse, fearing that I would be too late. Having my horse I, with my wife, soon mounted and went forward as fast as I thought the horse would bear. We hastened as if we were fleeing for our lives, all the while fearing that we should be too late to hear the sermon . . .

'When we came within about half a mile of the road to Middleton I saw before me a cloud of fog rising. I first thought it came from the river; but as I came nearer I heard a noise like a low rumbling of thunder and presently found it was the noise of horses feet coming down the road, and I could see men and horses slipping along in the cloud like shadows. The riders at scarcely a horse length behind each other, all in a lather and foamed with sweat. Every horse seemed to go with all his might to carry his rider to hear news from heaven for the saving of souls. It made me tremble to see the sight.'

When Cole and his wife got near the actual preaching place he said, 'I looked towards the river and saw the ferry boats running swift backwards and forwards, bringing over loads of people. Everything, men, horses and boats seemed to be struggling for life. The land and banks over the river looked black with people and all the twelve miles along I saw no man at work in his field, all seemed to be gone to the preaching. When I saw Mr Whitefield come upon the scaffold he looked almost angelical; a young, slim, slender youth, before some thousands of people with a bold undaunted countenance. It solemnized my mind, and put me into a trembling fear before he began to preach, for he looked as though he was clothed with authority from the great God, and a sweat, solemn solemnity sat upon his brow. And my hearing his preach gave me a heart wound by God's blessing.'

Whitefield's greatest triumphs in America were reserved for New England, where grew the spiritual and intellectual centre of the new world. In the September of 1740 he conducted a six-week tour which left the whole region of New England in a spiritual uproar. Unprecedented crowds numbering tens of thousands appeared from nowhere to hear the simple but dramatic message of spiritual rebirth and 'justification by faith alone'. One American writer has said that 'until George Washington, no colonial figure enjoyed greater popularity among the American populace'. He died in Newport, Rhode Island, on 15 October 1770, suddenly, as he had hoped he would, in the middle of a preaching tour.

Whitefield's influence has been a continuing one in the religious history of America. There, as in Britain, his influence was wholly for the good, and the destiny of which he had dreamt when he was a tapster in the Bell Inn in Gloucester, of something great awaiting him, was amply fulfilled.

SANKEY AND MOODY

(1837–99)

'Save All You Can'

In a small town in New England, USA, in the first part
of the nineteenth century, a man called Dwight L.
Moody was running a successful shoe business. But
things were stirring in that vast country which were
turning the hearts and minds of many people to the
spreading of the gospel across the Continent, as the
West was opened up by trade and exploration. The
preaching of the Word, as they saw it, to those new,
rough-and-ready communities out there was the
seed-bed of American evangelism which has such an
impact upon the shape of American christianity today,
and which continues to have an impact in the form of
influences coming over from America – Billy Graham
belongs directly to this tradition as we shall see in the
next chapter. Those early evangelistic meetings in the
growing United States were usually in the open air,
often within a circle of tents, which is why they were
often called 'tent meetings', and included as often as
not a fiery speaker accompanied by a solo singer and
popular hymns. The appeal was great, the influence
often very strong.

Dwight Moody, the one-time shoe salesman, was

much affected by this growing evangelism and soon took to it himself. He was never among those who went to the new frontiers in the West, but occupied himself at first around Chicago and eastwards towards New York. He had a moderate success; but already one notable development in his presentation had taken place. He had teamed up with a singing partner called Ira Sankey and the combination of the two was to prove sensationally effective as time went by.

This would not have been possible without one of the most striking developments which took place in America at around the same time – the birth of a popular American hymnody. Earlier generations of christians in America had often actively disapproved of hymns, like the puritans. After the revivals brought over the Atlantic by such men as George Whitefield, who used quite a lot of British hymns, especially those of the methodists, the whole temper changed. But it was the camp or tent meetings of the early evangelists which really set things going in this area. What was needed, and what they got, were simple popular tunes with easily-learned words. There had to be a pattern of verse and refrain which could be repeated over and over again. Some of the words came from British sources, some of the refrains owed a lot to the rhythms of the folk music of the Blacks. All this was greatly helped by the fact that, in the growing America of the day, singing, and particularly the singing of choruses, became a very popular pastime among many people. In the West, especially, the music teacher with his fiddle, and later, when things improved, the piano, became a familiar and important figure. All these developments made the way clear for the birth of a kind of popular religious music called gospel hymns. Simplicity of melody, chorus and words were essential and these soon became a prominent feature of the American evangelical scene. Hymns like 'Just As I Am' and 'What a Friend We have in Jesus', 'Rescue the Perishing', 'Pass Me Not, O Gentle Saviour', were soon topping the hymn-charts of the day. Ira Sankey, whom Moody took as his singing partner, became in this tradition about the best-known revival singer, enriching meetings with his splendid voice and dramatic presentation. His *Gospel Hymns* went through many editions and became well known on both sides of the Atlantic. So gospel hymns soon became a very important part of American evangelism and, indeed, of the christian personal life. They came from the people, and were sung by the people, and spoke of the people's direct devotional experience of Jesus Christ. Somewhere in them was a power of poetry which could sweep crowds along on, as one writer put it, 'billows and tides of heavenly emotion'.

It is not possible, without a look at this background of the emergence of the gospel hymn and the part Sankey played in it, to see in its real fullness the meaning of the remarkable story of Moody himself. His beginnings were very hard. The man who was to become the most noted evangelist of his age was born into poverty, one of nine children. His father died when he was four, leaving the whole family very badly off so that Moody at seventeen was sent away to work in his uncle's shoe-shop in Boston. There, in Sunday school, he was converted through one of his teachers, Edward Kimble. From there he went to Chicago and became a successful business-man on his own. But more importantly for this story, he became an active worker in his congregational church, undertaking, as he said, to fill four pews every Sunday with new recruits to the faith. This he actually did and by the time he was twenty-three he had founded his own Sunday school. He was not an intellectual, he was no scholar, but he was a great organizer and recruiter of new christians for others to teach. That was to be the pattern of his life, and who is to say there is anything wrong with that? Soon Moody was devoting himself full-time to this christian work, preaching to large crowds far and wide, always accompanied by his partner, the tall, bearded, impressively deep-voiced Ira Sankey.

Then the unexpected happened. Moody and Sankey together crossed the Atlantic to Britain on what they saw to be a quite modest preaching tour to which they had been invited. At first this did not go particularly well. Their methods and their whole approach were unfamiliar to British audiences. But, quite gradually, the shape of an enormous success began to emerge. Moody's preaching, his message which could be understood by the simplest, combined with the powerful effect of Sankey's songs and music and the gospel hymns, brought something new into British religious life. It was exciting, it could be understood by everybody. The two men became prodigiously popular, so much so that their tour in Britain lasted, instead of only a few months, for two full years, from 1873 to 1875.

The simplicity of Moody's message exactly fitted the needs of so many people who, living in the new industrial cities, had long been divorced from any kind of popular appeal in their religious lives. People in their thousands would listen with rapt attention as Moody spoke, for instance, of his famous 'Three Rs: Ruined by Sin, Redemption by Christ, and Regeneration by the Holy Ghost'. He used to say that the saving of souls was his goal, first and foremost. He used also to say that this was immensely urgent because the world in which those souls lived was in a terrible state. He said: 'I look upon this world as a wrecked vessel. God has given me a life boat and said to me: "Moody, save all you can".' At the heart of his message was a conviction that the world would never be put right until Jesus came again and founded his kingdom on earth. It was therefore immensely important and urgent to get as many people 'saved' as possible in time for this second coming. From this came the phrase which he used over and over again, 'save all you can'.

By the time Sankey and Moody returned to the United States from their resoundingly successful

British tour, they were national heroes on both sides of the Atlantic. Britain never forgot them, and their influence lasted a long time. In a way, it blazed the trail for American evangelists coming over from the States to Britain, just as Billy Graham has done. Back in the States Moody devoted himself to conducting revival campaigns, all of them marked by the extremely able organization and general back-up which, in this present day, continues to be a feature of the Billy Graham campaigns. So Moody and Sankey had a lasting effect upon the whole shape of modern evangelism which, in recent years, has been having a very big comeback.

There was, however, a lot more to Moody than great popular successes in massive revivalism. He and his followers truly believed in the urgency of the work they were doing and in its importance, and in the fact that there was not sufficient in modern life to give the human soul the inspiration which it needed. Only Christ could do that, and the time in which it was going to be possible was running out. That was the ultimate conviction. It was needful, therefore, to train more and more people, men and women, for the evangelistic efforts. In Chicago Moody adopted a bible institute, later and to this day called the Moody Bible Institute, whose purpose it was to train laymen for evangelistic efforts. Out of this and the conferences which he held near his home, grew an astonishingly huge missionary effort called the Student Volunteer Movement which had as its motto 'Evangelization of the World in this Generation'.

The story of that is remarkable in itself. The SVM, as it came to be called, had as its purpose the recruiting of people to go abroad as foreign missionaries, carrying the gospel. The emphasis was chiefly upon college students, and they were sought for by the SVM in the United States and in other countries as well. Thousands of college graduates signed a pledge to become a foreign missionary, 'if God permit'. That was a get-out clause for those who did not in fact go the whole way. But many did. By 1920 more than eight thousand who had joined the SVM had actually sailed abroad as foreign missionaries, more than two and a half thousand of them into China alone. Fifteen hundred went to India, nine hundred to Africa. But as time went by the emphasis changed, moving rather away from the direct preaching of the gospel to an interest in social concerns. And so the SVM, one of the most dramatic products from the inspiration of Moody, was seen to have had its day. But it had been a great day while it lasted; it had changed many lives and had called many to high endeavour.

Moody was a tireless and sincere evangelist, whose words with the songs of Sankey, made a mark on popular evangelism which will never fade away. Powerful, influential – his opposition to the doctrine of what was called baptismal regeneration, which he claimed the Church of England continued to teach –

reached the level of a national controversy, and three hundred thousand copies of the sermon he preached were sold. But always the basis of his fame was his preaching. Humour, common sense, a gift for epigram, were the very heart and centre of what he was and of his fame. His sermons were published every week until 1917, years after his death which took place in the South of France, at Mentone, in the January of 1892. So ended the greatest and the most popular preacher of his age; a very remarkable man.

CHARLES HADDON SPURGEON

(1834–92)

King of the Pulpit

Around the middle of the nineteenth century, one winter evening, a boy of sixteen stood up to preach in a room in a cottage near Cambridge. Immediately, without any obvious reason for it, he was seen not only as something way out of the ordinary, but as a youth of extraordinary potential. There was something about his manner, even more something about his voice, which attracted instant attention. The matter of his sermon was also very good indeed, far beyond what might have been expected for someone of his years. The only snag was his appearance. He was a plain youth, just as he was as a man, rather fat, with a large oval face topped by a black hair parted in the middle. This was Charles Haddon Spurgeon, destined to be the most popular and greatest preacher of his age, a true king of the pulpit if ever there was one.

There was something about that particular age which seemed to produce star preachers, although none were quite to acquire the amazing celebrity of Spurgeon. Whitefield had been gone nearly a hundred years when Spurgeon came on the scene. The eighteenth century was dead, and the excitements of early methodism and of the Wesleys and Whitefield himself had settled down to a general acceptance. But preaching, long before the days of radio or television or a popular press, was far and away the most popular means of communication. Given the man, given the message, given even the pulpit, a really able speaker could attract thousands. So the stage was set for the emergence of Spurgeon when he came on the scene. The stage was set in another way, also; his father and his grandfather had both been independent ministers used, in their own ways, to the art of this kind of public speaking. Spurgeon himself was converted while listening to a primitive preacher, a local methodist in the January of 1850. He was baptized and became a village preacher in Cambridgeshire. This was around the time when he stood up and astonished everybody in the room of that cottage, and in a few years he had left his methodist connections and was launched into a career which was to make him the most celebrated Victorian baptist preacher, becoming, by virtue not only of what he said but by his manner of saying it, a true media figure of his day.

Spurgeon was of Dutch origin, born at Kelvedon in Essex and for a little while an usher, or schoolmaster, in Newmarket – all this long before he was twenty – and then he became pastor to a small baptist congregation at nearby Waterbeach. But this was only the beginning. He was still only nineteen when he became the baptist pastor at the new Park Street chapel in Suffolk, south of the river in London. This was where things really took off. It had been a virtually empty chapel. Soon it was filled by people who had come to hear this astonishing new preacher who, with his directness and plain and homely message wrapped round with great eloquence, was filling the place. Some, even at that early stage, found some of what he said a bit too much for them: irreverent and vulgar by their standards. But none could deny his real power. Few realized, possibly not even Spurgeon himself, that he was standing at the beginning of a long line of famous preachers who were to make a mark on christian history in Britain, and in America particularly, right through the nineteenth century and well into the twentieth. Sankey and Moody, the evangelists who had already come over the Atlantic and were active in Britain in Spurgeon's day, were among them. But later and great figures were to be men such as John Clifford, Hugh Price Hughes, James Martineau. Beyond them again were to be people like Silvester Horne, Luke Wiseman, Dinsdale Young, Scott Lidgett, Tounley Lord, Lesley Wetherhead and many others. The line, in fact, extends right through to Billy Graham in this present day with his capacity for filling a stadium with people hanging on his words.

Here is a description of one of these great preachers in action: 'He tried the most daring flights, and never faultered, for tone and gesture were always right. Every word was given its due emphasis and carried its proper weight. Southern Whispers, Southern pause, a rapid rush of sentences then a crescendo. All this was studied. This vastly increased the force of the appeal.' That, which could with truth be said of Billy Graham today, was in fact said of Spurgeon himself.

Quite soon the new Park Street chapel in Suffolk was not big enough to hold him: before long he had moved on to the famous Exeter Hall, one of London's largest auditoriums. Even this had to be enlarged and while this work was in progress, Spurgeon daringly moved to the Surrey Gardens music-hall, a large and popular theatre where he preached from the stage to packed audiences of men and women.

This was very severely criticised. Many people, and quite sincerely, felt it absolutely wrong that a man should be preaching the gospel in a place where the stage-shows put on were quite often of a kind which some people found markedly off-colour. True enough, the Victorian music-hall could be, and frequently was, of a fairly raw kind of entertainment. How on earth could you mix this with religion? was the question which many people asked: they came up with answers sharply hostile to Spurgeon who was trying to do, and succeeding in doing, that very thing. There were times when he had an audience of ten thousand people in the Surrey Gardens music-hall and held them. So he became a real media figure of his day; the papers discussed him, some praised, some blamed; he was a real talking-point. And sometimes this enormous fame brought its own dangers. There was an occasion when someone started a false fire-alarm when he was preaching in the music-hall. In the panic which followed seven people were trampled to death and many injured. Spurgeon himself, standing on the stage, escaped; but it was a shaking experience. It was also the origin of a sarcastic story which was going the rounds years later of a famous preacher who was asked what he would do if he was speaking in a theatre and the place caught fire. His reply was that he would use all his eloquence to persuade people to keep their seats and be calm and then survive himself by walking through them and making his escape. But this, like many other criticisms, was quite unfair to Spurgeon. He had a message, and he had the manner of putting it across, and he had vast energy. His message was about living in the world as God wanted you to live, of trying always in daily life to live as if Jesus Christ were with you. His sermons were full of such phrases as a 'fall from grace', 'desire earnestly the best gifts', 'press towards the mark', 'the blood of Jesus', being 'sustained by the hope of eternal life', 'the endless mercies of God'. This kind of preaching was rather like prophesying in the Old Testament. It was full of the sense of the kind of adventure of being with God every moment of the day, and everything one should try to do and to be, and this kind of thing reached out with power into the lives of countless thousands of men and women.

So by the age of twenty-two Spurgeon was by far

the most popular preacher of his time. And then in 1861 the great metropolitan tabernacle in Newington Causeway was opened, with the capacity, almost always filled, of six thousand. In that place Spurgeon ministered until his death thirty-one years later.

During those years he established a position as a king of the pulpit unequalled in his day and age. But that was not all. In association with the metropolitan tabernacle some very important works were undertaken which made it one of the great centres of religious activity. The pastor's college which he founded, for instance, trained almost nine hundred men for the baptist ministry. There was also an orphanage set up for boys and girls. He inaugurated a society for the distribution of christian literature. He even had a monthly magazine called *The Sword and the Trowel* which reached a large circulation in its time. Surgeon was also himself a prolific author, and many editions of his books were sold, such as *The Saint and His Saviour, Morning by Morning, Evening by Evening*, and many others. In general, Spurgeon was good on social questions, showing a real concern for some of the great issues of the day, especially those which affected the condition of the poor and the outcast and the destitute – all those, in fact, who represented the dark side of Victorian prosperity.

G. A. STUDDERT KENNEDY
(Woodbine Willie)
(1883–1929)

Apostle of the Back Streets

Woodbine Willie, so nicknamed by troops in the First World War because of his habit of giving out cigarettes of that name to them, was an extraordinary man who made a great impact on his day. Now he is beginning to come back into the picture of things because so many of the evils he fought against, chiefly war and unemployment, have returned to the modern scene. To those who knew him he was a modern-day saint, and to those who listen to what he has to say now, the same impression comes through. 'The biggest little man of our day' was how he was described by Dick Sheppard, a famous Vicar of St Martin-in-the-Fields Church, London. Woodbine Willie was a small man, only five-foot-six. But he was a giant among men, able to mix on their level and speak on their wavelength to all and sundry. He shared the anxieties, fears and disappointments of common people. His life was devoted to suffering humanity. He was the back-street apostle, the disciple in the slums, a missionary of hope amid poverty and unemployment and war. He became the most celebrated of army-chaplains of all time. But he was a great deal more than that. He was a poet, and a prophet, a great campaigner in the years after World War I for economic and social justice, and one who had a magnetic attraction whenever he spoke.

His audiences were often the unemployed and the underprivileged. But he also spoke to the captains and kings of this world and they listened gladly. His potent mix of humour, indignation at injustice, and his comeplling christian message brought flocking around him both the shabby and the poor, and the wealthy. The magic of his personality got to the hearts and minds of men and women. Many took their first steps towards christian belief through his example. In his day, and in his particular manner, he was as much a witness for God, a great evangelist, as people like Grimshaw, and also, in his own particular style, a very great preacher and speaker like Spurgeon in his day. He was also a man who, because he exhausted himself to death, died for his faith and was a martyr to the circumstances in which he lived, as much as, many years later, the Polish priest Jerzy Popieluszko.

Geoffrey Studdert Kennedy was born the son of a clergyman in a poor parish in Leeds. When, after a period as a schoolmaster, he was himself ordained, he went to Rugby as a curate. This is where his unconventional manner and strange unorthodox talk began to raise eyebrows. He was no great respecter of persons and he was drawn to the poor, regularly found in the poor quarters of the town or in the back streets, holding court with lodging-house tramps and others of the down-and-out. He could go into the roughest of pubs and hold the company spellbound by one of his songs which he would sing in his Irish brogue. When he reached France some years later as a padre, he was to do exactly the same thing among troops who came to love him with a rare intensity.

But the war had not begun when he first went to the city of Worcester as vicar of a very poor parish, St Paul's; a place made up of a patchwork of back-to-back terraces and slums. It was a bad place at a bad time. There would be one toilet to every twelve houses. The little work there was very hard and unemployment and poverty were rife. This was the place where, when Studdert Kennedy arrived, he said that he wanted to be a friend to everyone. That was the beginning of a remarkable ministry. He was endlessly – some thought foolishly – generous, once actually giving away his own bed to an old man who did not have one. He would preach in the streets, talk in the pub, visit every home. He organized two soup kitchens, and was constantly seeking out help for those in need. People responded to him in a rare way and soon the red-brick church of St Paul's was filled with people.

Then, in 1914, came the First World War. At first it was not seen to be the massive tragedy it later turned out to be. Geoffrey Studdert Kennedy did not see it as a tragedy at the beginning, either, but went off as a padre with great enthusiasm. One of his earliest letters from the front-line describes Christmas Day, 1915. He conducted his first make-shift service in the square of a French village with the congregation of four hundred mud-covered and rain-soaked troops. They sang *Come All Ye Faithful* with all their might, and holy communion was celebrated in a large shed. He wrote: 'It was wonderful, no lights, no ritual, nothing to help but the rain and the far off role of guns, and Christ was born in a cattle shed on Christmas Day.'

Yet soon the horror and the brutality of this war – and of any war – got through to him. Maybe the process started when he was posted as a padre in one of the towns behind the lines, Rouen, where he would see, night after night, troop-trains taking young men off to the front, usually to be killed. That was when he used to, as he put it in another letter, 'slip out and arm myself with two knapsacks, one full of Woodbines and the other full of New Testaments. I would begin at the top of the train and work down it going into each carriage, the knapsacks on my back growing lighter, and the lump in my throat growing bigger. Often I would have to cling on to reach the last carriages, creeping along the footboards as the train began to move. At last I am left alone, sometimes with tears welling in my eyes, looking after the disappearing tail lights. There is nothing glorious about this. It is all sordid and filthy. God only knows the hardships these men endure on these journeys in packed, dirty carriages. No place to wash, no place to move, they sit and wait for eighteen hours or more, until, when, I suppose, they hear the far off sound of guns and know that the end is near.'

It was during these years that Studdert Kennedy accidently achieved fame by the poems which he wrote. No one had ever come across quite this kind of thing before, certainly not from a padre. Here is one:

> Waste of blood, and waste of tears,
> waste of youth's most precious years,
> waste of ways the Saints have trod,
> waste of glory, waste of God.

> War!

There were plenty more. They came out in a book called *Rough Rhymes* which had an enormous sale; typically, Studdert Kennedy gave the proceeds to charity. These verses, written in the kind of dialect in which most ordinary soldiers spoke in those days, had a great impact. Many people had begun to wonder where God and Jesus could be found in the frightful world which had emerged as the war went on. There is some suggestion of an answer in this piece of verse, describing how some stretcher-bearers go out into the mud to pick up a wounded man:

> Easy does it – bit of trench 'ere,
> mind that blinkin bit of wire,
> there's a shellow on your left there,
> lift him up a little igher . . .
> 'Ere we are now,
> stretcher case, boys,
> bring him out a cup of tea!
> In as much as ye have done it,
> Ye have done it unto me.

Thousands of people came to feel that Woodbine Willie, Geoffrey Studdert Kennedy, was expressing for them what so many wanted to say, that somehow, in some place, God was still to be found in the world and that, though the search for him was hard, and finding of him through faith was still certain. The great thing was to bet your life on the truth of this. As Studdert Kennedy put it in another of his verses:

> How do I know that God is good? I don't.
> I gamble like a man,
> I bet my life,
> upon one side in life's great war . . .

And again:

> Peace does not mean the end of all our striving.
>   Joy does not mean the drying of our tears;
> peace is the power that comes to souls arriving,
>   Upto the light where God himself appears.

After the war, in which he had won the Military Cross for gallantry in the field, Studdert Kennedy returned home a sadder and a wiser man. By this time he was very famous and people came to hear him for his wisdom and his counsel, from all over the land. The King made him a royal chaplain. But he felt that fame was no good for him and that his work was not done. As he had served to the utmost of his ability those who had suffered in war, now he felt pledged to serve to the utmost of his ability those who were suffering from the economic ills which followed the war, particularly from poverty and unemployment. This is when he became a christian socialist and a missioner for the Industrial Christian Fellowship. This was a body which existed to offer an embassy of goodwill, as they put it, among the industries of our land. It was just the kind of work, speaking at street-corners and to great crowds, which Studdert Kennedy excelled in. It was exhausting; the comrades were testing; but it was most effective because always he preached the love of Christ and the healing power of his Way at a time when most people were bitter and disillusioned. For the next seven years of his life – the last seven, as it happened – he was to travel continually all over Britain and overseas, preaching christian compassion mixed with fierce denunciations of the injustices of modern life. His retreats and crusades for the christian fellowship took him on a regular round of factory canteens, town-squares, street-corners, and cathedrals and major platforms alongside other great speakers of his day such as William Temple and Dick Sheppard. His power was extraordinary. There was one occasion when, at the end of a lunchtime address at London's Strand Theatre, the audience invaded the stage in emotional fervour to congratulate him. No one had ever seen anything like it. It is arguable that no one has ever seen anything like it since. But he took a realistic view of the apathy of the modern world just the same. That was what evoked one of his most famous poems of all, which is called *Indifference*!

When Jesus came to Golgotha they hanged him
    on a tree;
they drove great nails through hands and feet,
    and made a Calvary;
they crowned him with a crown of thorns,
    red were his wounds and deep,
for those were crude and cruel days,
    human flesh was cheap.
When Jesus came to Birmingham they
    simply passed him by,
they never hurt a hair of him,
    they only let him die;
for men had grown more tender,
    and they would not give him pain,
they only just passed down the street
    and left him in the rain.
Still Jesus cried, "forgive them,
    for they know not what they do".
And still it rained the wintery rain
    that drenched him through and through;
the crowds went home and left the streets
    without a soul to see,
and Jesus crouched against the wall
    and cried for Calvary.

Many people felt, and do now as he is being
rediscovered, that he was a true prophet. Others that
he was even like Christ himself in his utter self-giving.
And yet there was a lighter side to Studdert Kennedy.
He was extremely absent-minded. He would leave all

kinds of possessions around. On one occasion he had to rush back to his study because he had forgotten to put in his teeth. On another he went to a distinguished service wearing only football shorts under the robes of a royal chaplain. But he was a marvellous speaker, with a marvellous message of the love of God. He continued to write his books, including more wonderful verse. He was in constant demand all over the country, and also abroad. But he was wearing himself out; as his friends had always known that he would. He died, utterly exhausted, in 1929 in the middle of one of his missions. Strangely enough he felt that he had been a failure, but, as some pointed out, so did Christ seem to think for a moment on the cross! His message, at all times, was particularly strong for those who were groping towards a faith. To them he would say: 'The world and the life of men have meaning and purpose. At its heart the world is not mad, but sane. That is the bare minimum of faith for man. If that goes, everything goes, we can neither live nor think about Christ, but only take a long time to die.' His words were once well described as 'the unrestrained utterances of a soul in revolt'.

But, if he felt himself a failure, the world did not. At his funeral service the preacher, his friend the Dean of Worcester, said that 'He, like St Paul, was in journeyings off, suffering from fatigue, facing dangers, and often rousing antagonism by his plain-speaking and refusal to talk platitudes. He gave health and strength and all his powers of mind and speech to bring men and women everywhere to see in the cross the salvation of the world.' Above all, he took conventional religion out into the street, put it to the test there and found it meaningful. As he once said: 'Nobody worries about Christ as long as he can be kept shut up in churches. He is quite safe inside. But there is always trouble if you try and let him out.' There was plenty of trouble when Studdert Kennedy did just that; but it was a glorious trouble, and he has been and will be remembered for it because he was one of the great witnesses for God.

BILLY GRAHAM

(1918–   )

Prophet of Hope

One evening in 1934 in a place called Charlotte in
North Carolina there was a real, old-style, tent-
meeting evangelistic mission in progress. This was
something in the tradition of all those mission
preachers who had travelled over middle and western
America since the middle of the last century. On this
occasion the missioner was a man called Fowler Ham,
who had been brought over from Louisville to inspire
in the farming people a christian message in the midst
of the great depression they were going through.

The tent and the speaker's platform were actually
situated on a farm belonging to a man called Frank
Graham. The setting was as crude as the rhetoric
which came from the plank-floored platform; even the
aisles were covered with sawdust to lay the mud which
these farming people had brought in from the fields.
And yet, night after night throughout the mission
people packed in, often more than five thousand at a
time, filling every seat. The tent had open walls so that
the people could bring boxes and sit on the edge of the
crowd, listening.

Among them was a teenage boy called Billy

Graham, the son of the farmer who owned the land where the mission was taking place. He had not at first thought much of the mission until he heard the preacher take out of his text, 'For God so loved the world, that he gave his only begotten son, but who-so-ever believeth in him shall not perish, but have everlasting life.' Somehow this got under the skin of the young Billy and made him think. The next night he turned up again with a friend. The preacher, in his usual dramatic manner, started off by suddenly announcing: 'there is a great sinner in this place tonight'. It was quite a usual ploy with him; he did it every night. On this occasion the words reached right into the soul of the teenage boy listening, so much so that, at the end of the meeting when members of the audience were invited to go forward and make them-selves known as those who accepted God and Christ, the young Billy turned to his friend suddenly and said 'let's go'. So they did, and Billy Graham was, for the first and last time, converted. It was the last time because it never needed to happen again. The most successful evangelist of the twentieth century from that moment began a career which has had no looking back. When he spoke about it afterwards, when he was famous worldwide, Billy Graham said 'It was as simple as that, and as conclusive. There were no tears, no blazing voices, no gift of tongues. Have you ever been outdoors one day when the sun suddenly breaks through the clouds? Deep inside, that is how I felt. The next day, I am sure I looked the same. But to me everything looked different. I was finding out for the first time the sweetness and joy of God, and being truly born again.'

Billy Graham had been born on the farm at Charlotte, North Carolina. His father and mother brought him up very strictly, both parents being members of the local presbyterian church. It was a time and a place of strong evangelism, converting, repentance-provoking, even bible-thumping. The Graham family, though ardent in their faith, were no wild-eyed fanatics but sensible. Billy had been brought up in this way. What had been lacking was the spark of conversion. And that came at the tent meeting on that night in 1934. He used to say that he found a text in the Bible that night which was to guide him ever afterwards: 'Being confident in this very thing, that he which hath began a good work in you will perform it, until the day of Jesus Christ, (Philippians 1.6). But there is more to the story of Billy Graham than that. It has not been by accident, nor without enormous labour and continuing faith, and many challenges, that he has become far-and-away the most famous evangelist of this day, or perhaps even of any other. Because of radio and television and air-travel he has been able to make a global impact far beyond anything ever reached by any of his predecessors. In his hundreds of crusades he has been seen by more people than any other human in history; it has been claimed, by over fifty million. He has travelled worldwide, met nearly everyone of importance on the public scene, acted as adviser to every American president since Truman. He has received many honours – the reason for his title of doctor is that he has received four honorary degrees of that nature from various universities in America. When a paper called *The Christian Century* ran a poll to find out who was the best-known religious leader, Billy Graham came first by a long margin.

Some of the stages of his rise to such global fame have been remarkable. One of the most important of these was when, in 1949, he conducted a tent revival – mission in Los Angeles. This caught the attention of the famous press magnate, William Randolph Hearst. Because this man got the idea that Graham was campaigning against communism, which was by no means entirely the case, he gave orders that all his papers should support Graham by national publicity. This really launched Billy Graham on the public scene, at any rate in America. Twenty-one years later he was conducting several campaigns a year. Maybe even more importantly, he was reaching millions of people through a nine hundred-station radio network, through several special television programmes every year, and publishing a magazine called *Decision* with a circulation of over four million. In addition to all this he was running a syndicated column in many newspapers.

The statistics about Billy Graham continue to be astonishing. He has conducted two hundred 'crusades for Christ'. He has made over two hundred visits to Europe, Asia, Africa and Australia. Over fifty million people have seen him during these crusades. Millions more have heard him and seen him on radio and television. One and-a-half million have made their commitment to Christ through him. His crusades in Britain alone have been very remarkable occasions; perhaps the most significant religious events of our times in the sense that, as a christian, he has been able to attract more attention to his message than anybody else.

What is that message? His great success always seems to have rested upon a clear and simple evangelistic appeal to accept Christ, to take Christ into one's life, to devote everything to Christ, and to follow the teaching of the Bible. He is absolutely convinced that the world will not be a better place, nor will the people in it be able to lead rich and full lives, until this vital decision for Christ has been made. The essential simplicity of this message has never changed over the years and continues basically the same to this day.

Certain elements in his appeal are important to the impact he makes. His appearance, for one thing, is impressive; six-foot-two high with a handsome face and light-blond hair, and blue eyes, deep-set and brilliant. He has great personal charm. His voice is appealing, his teaching is plain and simple. He also has the ability to transmit the message of the scriptures into terms of everyday life and into contemporary situations. He is personally very humble, his belief in Jesus and the Bible is basic and is seen to be. He also seems able to implant in those who hear him a belief that mankind's problems, however complex the world we live in, come ultimately from disobedience to God's laws but that, because of Christ's atoning sacrifice on the cross, men and women are nevertheless able to live new lives in him and with him, however difficult and challenging the world.

Billy Graham has had many critics, and continues to have. There are some who point to the lavish build-up of his crusades with the prestigious organization behind him, the mass choirs, the gifted singers, the staginess of the presentation of Graham himself. But this, of course, lies much in the tradition of that type of American mission-evangelism which lies behind him. Others criticized Billy Graham's close friendship with President Nixon who ended his term of office with the scandal of Watergate. But no one has ever accused Graham of any personal dishonesty in that or in any other field. Perhaps a more serious criticism, as always, comes from the more intellectual, who believe that the extreme simplicity of his message is simply inadequate to meet the problems and the needs of such a highly complex world as the present. Is the old bible-message of salvation, in fact able to sand up in a time when man is one the one hand reaching into space and on the other possessed with such knowledge that he can destroy the world? There are those who think not and who judge Billy Graham as a light-weight among the heavy-weight problems of the age.

And yet, when all the criticisms have been made, the fact remains – and it is a fact – that Billy Graham has reached out with his message, however simple it may be, into the minds and hearts of more people than any other person of his kind, probably ever. Modern technology may have helped him to do this: the fact remains he has done it, and continues to do it. As one commentator has said: 'Graham has been a major force in Evangelical Christianity throughout the world through the work of the Billy Graham Evangelistic Association and through his support of such Evangelistic Institutions as Christianity Today . . . And even in the nineteen-eighties, he seems as committed as ever to preach the Gospel throughout the world, his popularity undiminished, his audiences still large and enthusiastic . . . No other religious figure has come close to rivalling the popularity and prestige of Billy Graham.'

What are the kind of things he has been saying all these years? Here are some examples: 'When you come to know Christ, there dwells within you the holy spirit, who gives you supernatural strength to overcome temptation and evil, so that when you face it, you don't face it alone. The spirit of God gives you the power to say no.' 'There are evidences of a lost sense of sin in modern life. It is evident in the

56

increase of profanity and obscenity. Our deprived speech is a direct reflection of our deprived lives. Our lost sense of sin is evident in our accent on pleasure. The hue and cry of today is "Let us eat, drink and be merry, for tomorrow we die". We are becoming a nation of playboys and are debasing the wisdom God has given us upon the altars of appetite and desire. We are becoming wise to do evil.' 'We are rich in the things which perish, but poor in the things of the spirit. We are rich in gadgets, but poor in faith. We are rich in goods, but poor in grace. We are rich in know-how, but poor in character. We are rich in words, but poor in deeds. We say we are rich, but in God's estimate we are wretched, miserable, poor, blind and naked.' Such is the voice of one who is, without a doubt, and whatever his critics may say, one of the most significant religious leaders of our times.

DAVID WATSON

(1933–84)

The Man who Walked with God

In the early nineteen-seventies it was clear to many that remarkable things were happening at the church of St Michael-le-Belfrey in York. This church had, as a matter of fact, been scheduled for closure so that it could be converted into a museum for the York Minster standing on the other side of the road. But then a young man called David Watson went there as vicar. He had already had some notable years at another church in York, St Cuthbert's, but this had become too small for the congregation that had grown around his work, and St Michael-le-Belfrey provided an answer. Soon the church had become the centre for a vivid christian life of a new kind, of a very twentieth-century kind, made possible by the personality of David Watson but always focused through him on God and on God's power.

Here was a man – a young man – standing in the long tradition of witnesses for God, evangelists of many different sorts and conditions from George Fox through Whitefield, Spurgeon and Studdert Kennedy to Billy Graham, and yet, though strongly in that tradition, David Watson was different in his method and approach. Just how different was observed by a group of investigators who, in the name of the Archbishop's council on evangelism, visited St Michael's towards the end of 1977 with the object of finding out what was really going on. One of this group described an evening service: 'David Watson preaches. Not only the service, but the whole life of the congregation hinges upon this fact. He is a crisp, careful preacher . . . His illustrations are from personal experience, or from his wide reading, or from the newspaper. There are no dramatics, little rhetoric. The basic style is plain teaching. That the spirit is in it you do not doubt. There is no attempt to work up an atmosphere.' The same observer goes on to ask why, in view of this fairly temperate approach, is the atmosphere so electric? 'Prayer is one clue . . . Prayer is obviously the warp and woof of the whole process, prayer that expects God's answers, and knows that he expects this of his children. Beyond that it hardly needs saying that David Watson is a gifted person. He is a talented Evangelist and expositor, moreover, he knows his people so well that he speaks convincingly to them, as part of the one body which is doing the one job together.'

At the communion, he went on to say, people moved up to the front of the church in great numbers. A liturgical dance – the use of mime and music and drama, all valuable parts of David Watson's ministry – had just been concluded. Now all received the bread and wine of the sacrament. Some stayed behind for a healing laying-on of hands. There was a warm and loving atmosphere among the crowd. After the service there was much talk and fellowship together; everyone was aware of belonging to a church which somehow had given birth to a novel kind of fellowship. It was never a matter of a 'Sunday only' experience; all were united together in various church-based christian enterprises throughout the week. Some, in fact, lived together in what were called 'households', married or single, with children or without, but all striving to follow the ideal of the apostles in having all things in common. Here was a church which was, in practice, a large extended family in which lay people of many kinds fulfilled many different functions. There were elders responsible for groups all over the city. Everyone who had a hand in this was called upon to work hard and devote much of his, or her, life to serving the Lord Jesus in their particular sphere, always members of the one family in him. It was an ideal which inevitably brought many tensions and not a few difficulties, but it was nevertheless certainly the case that very remarkable movements of the spirit were going on in those years at St Michael-le-Belfrey.

The observer who was sent to take a look at all this ended his account of the evening service by saying: 'The corporate nature of the Evangelistic impact of St Michael-le-Belfrey is witnessed to by many who have come to a personal relationship with Christ there, and from it we learn one of the greatest lessons of David Watson's ministry. When at some point in the service

David reminds those who have never come to Christ that he is waiting for their response, one sees that he is only putting into words that which is already evident in the lives and attitudes of those who are worshipping God together.'

David Watson was brought up in a strict evangelical family and after attending St John's College, Cambridge, went to Ridley Hall. He was then a curate in Gillingham, after which he went to Holy Sepulchre, known as the round church, in Cambridge, and then to St Cuthbert's in York before going to St Michael's where the work of his ministry emerged and developed, touching so many lives. This may sound like a conventional success story but it was more profound than that. Here was a man absolutely convinced that he knew God, that God knew him and that they could talk together, and, what is more, that God had something specific for him to do, as he has for everybody. The main purpose of life is to find out what that is and to carry it out.

Some felt that the strictness of his upbringing might have made David Watson somewhat narrow at the beginning of his ministry, but many events were soon to come together and move in such a way that his horizons were dramatically enlarged. He was to discover that anybody who, in the name of Christ, sought to love and serve people with such intensity was bound to suffer in the process and be challenged at many points. In the life of the parishes where he served, David Watson was able to develop what was, in many ways, a new idea of the total involvement of all church members in a common life and endeavour together. He was able to develop new ideas in worship and liturgy. He was able to practise and encourage a healing ministry, and many experienced physical healing through his ministry. Strange and exciting phenomena, associated by many with the life of the early church, happened around him; speaking with tongues, direct answers to prayer, a blazing adventure of faith all along the line.

There was nothing simple about David Watson. He was not only a very gifted preacher, he was also a highly successful writer. His books, *One in the Spirit, I Believe in Evangelism, I Believe in the Church, Is Anyone There?, Discipleship*, and, finally and most memorably, *Fear No Evil*, became and have remained best-sellers. 'David Watson', as another observer has said, 'was never merely David Watson. He was a carrier, like all great evangelists, of a message, and that message, of the love of God and of the challenge of God and of the reality of God, was destined to be proclaimed by him in many different situations.'

He was called to evangelistic efforts in many parts of the world. His 'Renewal Weeks' attracted participants in many countries; New Zealand, South Africa, Canada, the States, Norway and Sweden, and Eastern Europe, and his missions and festivals, under the auspice of the Belfry Trust, took him everywhere. The challenge of the situations in which he found himself, notably in Northern Ireland, affected his outlook, which broadened greatly. Through his involvement with the charismatic renewal movement he was brought into touch with many Roman Catholics, who were themselves drawn to this new experience of christian renewal. Some of his more narrowly-based evangelistic colleagues criticized him for this, but David had grown with the sense of the greatness of God's church so he could no longer maintain a narrow sectarian outlook. His relationships with christians of all churches in Ireland became particularly significant. He held a major mission in Belfast and Dublin in the November of 1983 when he was ill and failing. But many people were enriched by his message of peace and reconciliation in the name of Christ.

By this time he was already dying of the cancer which eventually killed him and, as it happened, his visit followed within a week of a frightful tragedy when an IRA gunman shot down members of the congregation of a little Pentecostal church on the border between Ulster and the Republic. It needed courage, it needed utter devotion, to preach, as David did, a message of love in such an atmosphere. He preached in a roman catholic church in the suburbs of Dublin. He preached in the Shankhill and the Falls areas of Belfast. He will not be forgotten there.

Here, it seemed, was a new figure arising with a

new power of God to speak to those who so badly needed such a message in the godless society of the modern world, but he was stricken by cancer. To many this seemed inexplicable. If David Watson was serving God so well, why was such a fate destined for him? The first and lasting reaction of his many followers was to pray for him. So a great wave of prayer on his behalf arose; could it not be that he who had healed so many through his prayers might be healed by the prayers of others? For a time there was a remission but eventually the disease closed in. Watson had moved to London from York in order to make himself freer for the great mission works which seemed to be lying before him, but on Saturday, 18 February 1984, he died. He had faced up to the challenge and the mystery of his illness and impending death and in his last book, in the epilogue, he wrote: 'Whatever else is happening to me physically, God is working deeply in my life . . . In that position of security I have experienced once again his perfect love, a love that casts out all fear.'

He was, said the Archbishop of York in an address at a thanksgiving service for David Watson, 'a burning and shining light'. 'He was this for the Church, and for the world and for people. He stood for a city set on a hill which cannot be hid. He stood for a lamp on a lamp stand, for the illumination of the world.' The secret of his ministry, the Archbishop said, was that, like St Paul, it was everything for him to live with Christ. The Archbishop ended

his address with these words: 'Perhaps David's greatest resource of all was that he knew that he would
go to his eternal home and find his Father waiting
for him'.

FATHER POPIELUSZKO

(1947–1984)

Through Death to Life

An astonishing sight can be seen any day, at almost any hour, outside the church of St Stanislaw Kostka in Warsaw. The church is not in the least beautiful, being raw and new. Its walls are usually decorated with banners of the banned trade union, Solidarity, in total defiance of the communist government of Poland. But what draws the crowds, which make an astonishing sight with their favour and size, is a grave. In that grave lies the body of a young priest called Jerzy Popieluszko, murdered by secret policy in 1984. Recently, when it was rumoured that the authorities intended to remove the body in order to lessen the crowds around the place, volunteers were called for to guard the grave in groups of four, day and night. So many came forward that a rota sufficient for two years was immediately forthcoming.

The story of this Polish Priest really cannot be understood without looking first at another story – the tragic and tumultuous history of Poland. Now part of the Soviet Bloc of Eastern European countries, the ancient kingdom of Poland, standing as it does between Germany on the one side and Russia

on the other, has always been a land in a state of
tension, threatened throughout history by powerful
neighbours and frequently occupied and over-run.
Gemany has conquered Poland in times past even
before the Second World War. Russia has conquered and occupied Poland many times in history,
and now does again. The country has been 'partiti-
oned', cut in half, divided up, shared out between
opposing and stronger forces time and again. All
these happenings have brought immense suffering
to the Polish people; they have been unconquerable,
they have always resisted with the full force of their
national character. Many, many thousands, down
the generations, have been killed, imprisoned, sent
into exile. In the Russia of the Tzars there were tens
of thousands of Poles, political prisoners in Siberia.
The German occupation of the Second World War
brought terrible suffering and millions of Poles
perished. The Soviet-Russian occupation, which still
continues, made worse by the fact that it is avowedly
atheist, has brought suffering untold. But always there
has been a force at work in Poland which has steeled its
people to resist and to endure in a continuing hope for
their land. This is their faith, which comes to them
through the catholic Church which is at the heart of
their situation, now as it always has been, and which is
the true custodian of the Polish soul. The present
pope, himself a Pole, said 'Poland's history cannot be
understood without Christ. The Polish people cannot
be understood without Christ.' This is the back-

ground to the story of Father Popieluszko.

Father Popieluszko was born in 1947 in a remote region of eastern Poland from which it is possible to see, not far away, the Soviet border. It is an area where many invading armies have marched and counter-marched throughout history. Not far away from the very farmstead where he was born is a forest containing the bodies of over four thousand people, including many priests and nuns, who resisted the Germans in their occupation. His parents were peasants, who were devout and practising catholics. Jerzy, their son, soon made it plain that he wished to join the priesthood and so, in 1965, he entered the Warsaw seminary to study. It was not an easy thing to do. Such young men were marked out for harsh treatment by the authorities because any practice of religion was seen as being in opposition to the prevailing communist power. This harassment could take many forms. One instance of it in Popieluszko's case was when he was doing his national service. One day he was found with a rosary in his hand and was ordered to throw it on the ground and tread on it with the threat that if he refused, he would be beaten and sent to the punishment cells. He did refuse and was so punished, but as this was merely one small incident, so small in the general pattern of things, he did not feel it necessary to mention it until years later when the tale came out.

Popieluszko was ordained in 1972 and was sent to the parish of Zabki, just outside Warsaw. Before long it became clear that he was delicate; the workload which he imposed on himself was too much and he collapsed, so it became necessary for him to enter hospital for a time. This proved a fruitful period because it brought him in touch with the medical world of doctors and nurses with whom, because he was a gifted priest, he soon formed very close relations. It was the beginning of much greater things to come.

In 1980 the workers of Poland rose up in yet another revolution in their country's history. It was a rising against an alien power and against a harsh communist party discipline, accompanied by gross injustice of treatment. These times saw the creation of Solidarity, the new union which was to have such power and to lead to so much. It also saw the burgeoning of a movement which had the Church at its very heart and which turned to the Church for much of its leadership. In its early stages this protest movement was crushed by the security police. Many workers were arrested, many imprisoned, many beaten up and tortured. This was the point at which Jerzy Popieluszko's deep involvement with the workers began.

The centre point of protest was the Lenin ship-yard at Gdansk, where a factory committee, led by the famous figure of Lech Walesa was confronting the authorities, an event which made world news at the time. Many other factories supported the Gdansk shipyard workers. Among the supporting factories was the Warsaw steel plant. Here the workers, occupying their plant, wished to find a priest who would celebrate Sunday mass for them. The man chosen, almost by chance as it seemed at the time, was Popieluszko. He said later: 'the memory of that Worker's Mass at the Warsaw Steel Plant will stay with me until I die. I went there jittering. This situation was absolutely new. What would I find there? How would the workers receive me? Who would do the readings? Who would sing the hymns? . . . And then at the gate I first began to feel astonished. The crowds of people smiling and crying at the same time and clapping. At first I thought that there was someone important behind me. But they were clapping me – the first priest in the history of this plant to enter at the main gate.'

This was the beginning of a close association in Christ with the workers of the steel works and, later, his influence spread throughout Poland. In time the strike which had triggered off the protest died away. But the workers asked Father Jerzy to be their chaplain and his church, St Stanislaw Kostka, became the centre of the chaplaincy of the Warsaw steel works. The priest also became closely associated with Solidarity, exercising a great influence, often calming down extremists and bringing spiritual and moral help to many. In addition, he formed a liaison between the church authorities in Poland, themselves going through an extremely difficult time, and those who had been or would be on strike. After the strike the government decided to declare martial law, following which many thousands of trade union members and their supporters were arrested and imprisoned, many in internment camps. Father Jerzy's work increased. He felt it was his duty to be with people in good times and bad; he felt it his duty to increase the sense of human rights and freedom of speech. He said: 'I felt perhaps that it was then that they needed me most, in those difficult times, praying for them in their prison cells, in the court rooms where I went to hear their trials.'

At this time he was living in one room at the parish house, a room which was littered with gifts which had come to him to pass on to the workers and especially their families who were in need. He worked throughout the day, beginning with an early mass and then occupying himself with constant contacts from dawn to dusk, distributing medicine and parcels, giving comfort and help. There was a constant procession of people into the single room he occupied, because it became known that he was open to all at all hours. 'Every day many people came who did not necessarily want material help', one observer recorded, 'they wanted to talk, they wanted someone to share their sorrows and tears with them, they wanted to share their troubles.'

But there were bad times coming for Father Popieluszko. On the night of 14 December 1982 a bomb was thrown into his small single room. He was not there, because he was out visiting at a local hospital; but the signs were clear: the authorities were going to get him. This was the point at which his influence burst with its full force upon Poland. He began to preach in St Stanislaw Kostka church a series of what became known as 'patriotic sermons'. These were immensely powerful declarations of the rights of all to freedom of action and belief, to freedom to worship in suffering Poland. The death penalty was introduced for anyone making anti-state pronouncements. But Popieluszko went on his way for it was ordained that he should. 'Because freedom of speech has been taken away from us by the introduction of Martial Law,' he said from the pulpit, 'let us, while listening to the voice of our heart and conscience, think of those brothers and sisters who have been deprived of their freedom.' They were words spoken by the right man at the right time in the right place. The response was enormous. One observer wrote, 'when Father Jerzy spoke, a unique silence would descend upon the enormous congregation. As a gifted orator he expressed fiercely the thoughts that others were unable or afraid to utter.' He said again: 'a nation with a thousand years of Christian tradition behind it will always seek full freedom. The yearning for freedom cannot be stopped without violence, as violence is the weapon of those who do not possess the truth. Man can be crushed by violence but not enslaved . . .'

There could be one end to this and it came on Friday 19 October 1984. Popieluszko's car, driven by a chauffer, was stopped in a forest as he was driving to a town in northern Poland to take part in a special mass for the working people. There were secret police in the car which had been following and then overtaken and stopped the priest's. The chauffeur, a man called Chrostowski managed to escape, which made all the difference because he was able to give testimony as to what had happened afterwards. But Popieluszko was captured, handcuffed and beaten. Later he was gagged, taken to a nearby reservoir and, with a stone tied around his legs, thrown into the water and drowned. It was not known for some time what had happened. But on the 29 October the Ministry of the Interior announced that the body had been taken out of the water and that the priest was dead. Few events, even in the history of tragically troubled Poland, have created so great a reaction. His body was taken back to St Stanislaw Kostka church and there buried in the grounds. This was the beginning of amazing scenes around the church which continue to this day. Those who had murdered him were arrested and, although the death sentence was demanded for them, they received instead long prison sentences.

The news of Father Popieluszko's murder shocked the world, as one friend testified: 'Many papers published a photograph of Father Jerzy', he wrote, 'showing this boyish figure of a priest with an expression of a very special kind of peace on his face – a peace not of this world. Weak in body but steadfast in spirit, Father Jerzy had fought for truth and justice in the country which he loved so dearly.

His only weapon had been prayer, and his leader was Christ himself.'

DAVID SHEPPARD

(1929–   )

Prophet of the Inner City

In every age God raises up people who emerge as
challenging voices presenting the gospel in word and
deed. These are people who are witnesses to God in
ways which particularly fit the age in which they live.
These are people who seem able to pick out the major
challenges of their times and to challenge the rest of the
world with them, refusing to accept its indifference to
the claims of God, and overcoming that indifference
by their own faith and energies. Such people are as true
prophets of this modern age as of any other.

One of these is David Sheppard, Bishop of Liverpool. The challenge he presents to all of us is to think
now and urgently about the problems of the inner
cities of our land, decaying areas of poverty and
underprivilege where, in recent years, such as at
Toxteth, Brixton, Tottenham and elsewhere, riots
have broken out. Often these have been caused by local
and immediate and passing causes. But underlying
them always is the deep anger felt by many of those,
especially the young and black unemployed, who live
in them, and the circumstances and the conditions
which, they feel, make them the victims of injustice.

And underlying this is the problem presented by the inner city itself. Once the heartlands of Britain's industrial past, they have tended to become the wastelands of Britain's industrial present, with the result that those left behind in them have tended to be forgotten and their needs overlooked. David Sheppard's essential message is that, in the name of the very gospel, we must all develop a concern for these areas and see what we can do to rebuild the waste places.

It would be difficult to find a less probable figure to be a prophet of these inner cities than David Sheppard. Born in 1929 and educated at Trinity Hall and at Ridley Hall, Cambridge, he seemed from the beginning a man born to a fortunate and privileged life. In his Cambridge days and later he was a first-class cricketer and captain of England in the test matches against Australia. This gave him an image which took quite a long time to grow away from; tall, handsome, a splendid athlete, he was universally popular right through his days as a curate in Islington. But then came the first of the developments in his life which removed from it for ever the image of the cricketing parson. In 1958 he was appointed warden of the Mayflower Family Centre in London's Canning Town, a place of pioneer social-christian work among the underprivileged. This had been a dockland settlement run at one time by Malvern College; but it had run down and David Sheppard wrote about its rebirth under its new name of the Mayflower Family Centre. He tells the story of this in the first book he ever wrote, called *Parson's Pitch*. The picture he gives is that of a warm and friendly neighbourhood scheme bringing in all kinds of people, especially the young, who had before had nothing to do with the christian faith whatever. He said: 'It is a maxim of ours that we cannot expect to talk to others about our faith in Christ unless we are prepared also to give them time and real friendship. It is also a maxim that, when someone has come to a clear faith in Christ, he should be given something to do in the service for his Lord . . . Christian work cannot be measured in numbers: our work can be gauged much better by listening in on a group of leaders sitting round on a Sunday evening.' All of those present, he added, were between eighteen and twenty-two. These were years of unspectacular but enormously fruitful work among people to whom the whole idea of the christian faith was entirely new. But it was often hard and challenging. As he said, 'If we didn't believe in God then we shouldn't have been involved in the work in the beginning. It was only the challenge my London neighbours presented to my Christian faith that drew me into it.'

Sheppard was there for eleven years, and then moved on, to the surprise of many, to become Bishop of Woolwich. Some wondered whether he would be able to measure up to what had been the very intellectual pattern set by his famous predecessor, John Robinson of *Honest To God* fame. But here, as in the Mayflower Family Centre, Sheppard brought his own particular gifts of warmth and christian love to bear upon the problems of the inner city as he found them in Woolwich, and they were plenty. These were the matters which he was going to bring into prominence as his life and authority developed. Already in Woolwich he was encountering, as he had at the Mayflower, not only poverty, not only loneliness, not only underprivilege of all kinds, but also complete indifference to anything which the Church and the christian faith represented. This was the real challenge and it has continued to be the real challenge for all that David Sheppard represents. He has never been tired of saying that the Church in all its different manifestations has failed, always, within the urban setting of streets and buildings in which the great majority of people live. His way of approach to this challenge has been not that of the evangelists with their vast congregations and their popular preaching, but rather to develop deep relationships with the few so that they, in their turn, could become disciples who would show something of what Jesus could mean by the quality of their lives. So at Woolwich, as at the Mayflower Family Centre, people found in Sheppard an inspiring example of how the christian faith can be lived today, however drab the circumstances surrounding it.

The scene widened when, in 1975, David Sheppard became Bishop of Liverpool. Here the problems and challenges he had been trying to face up to all through his ministry so far were presented in an acute form. Liverpool is a run-down city, as the world knows only too well, with its unemployment, its derelict docks, its great cathedral on the hill like a stranded whale, with the new roman catholic cathedral not far away. There was also, in Liverpool, a long tradition of religious intolerance, quite apart from the usual difficulties of poverty, bad housing, together with racial minorities presenting their own particular challenges. Within this situation it soon became clear that David Sheppard's horizons were widening very much. Because the conditions in which people lived had a profound effect upon their outlook it was never enough to try and present the gospel as something isolated from the rest of life. Houses mattered, drains mattered, street-lighting mattered, schools mattered, job opportunities mattered, so that practical concern for the physical condition of people's lives mattered enormously and was a proper area in which a man of God should be deeply involved.

There is one passage in a notable book which Sheppard produced about this time called *Built as a City, God and the Urban World Today*: 'Society today is expressed in urban living, so trying to understand what the big city does to people and what Christ's mission within it is not a marginal subject for Christians. Urban mission is one of the priorities today in God's work. If we fail here, if we ignore the city and its pressures, there is no gospel which we can preach anywhere else. . .' He went on to say something which has become increasingly noticeable in recent years, that some parts of some cities are the product of indifference and greed on the part of those in power. 'They are also the products of a fatalism, almost unconscious, on the part of good men who have given up the effort to make the city warm and human. The city traps people. Millions all over the world feel this. They then begin to feel that anything they think or say will never change anything. Christians who hope that people will make conscious, responsible choices to serve the living God must not withdraw from the complex issues of the city. They must commit themselves to help make it the liberating organism a city can be.'

But it has not been easy to hold such a vision against the background of the dark things which have happened in Liverpool, as elsewhere, in recent years, when the inner city has come to boiling point. This happened in the Toxteth area of Liverpool in the July of 1981. It seemed to begin when a young black man was stopped by a police car. A crowd gathered, more police arrived, and the rioting was on. It was very serious indeed; petrol bombs were used, whole areas went up in flames, and the police had to battle hard to contain the violence. One of the very few bright spots in all this darkness was the leadership given by the Church and its representatives throughout the whole area. It could have been one indication of the rioters' recognition of this that no churches were damaged and that in many places clergy were accepted as intermediaries between police and rioters. A frequently-seen figure in the streets at this time was David Sheppard together with his close friend, the roman catholic Archbishop of Liverpool. This again was an instance of the remarkable leadership which he has been able to give. In his time there has come about a healing of inter-church animosities on a scale which many would not have thought possible and which some people have difficulty in believing even now.

Sheppard's latest book *Bias to the Poor*, is some indication how far his thought has gone. The essence of it is that the Christian, as did Jesus himself, must love and serve and have a continuing concern for the underprivileged in our society. In particular he must do so whenever their sufferings are the product of the way in which the great cities of our times have gone wrong, as riots in other places since Liverpool have also shown. The essence of David Sheppard's belief is that the city can be put right, provided we go on believing in it. He says: 'Belief in the city of God which will be made perfect one day, leads me to say that God has a purpose for the big city now. Our programme must learn something from the terms of reference of Jesus' mission. Its marks are the mending of broken lives and the proclaiming of good news to the poor. He set himself alongside those who did not have influence with the authorities, with the victims of principalities and powers. He was a realist about the evil influences in the world, as we have to be if we are serious about winning some battles in the city. He expected no cheap victories. His way was through suffering and death to a resurrection which was only known to a minority. He promises that his resurrection is only the first fruits of a harvest to come.'

From George Whitefield, William Grimshaw, Charles Spurgeon, Sankey and Moody, even from Billy Graham, there is a long road to the very modern witness to the reality of God which comes through the lives of such very contemporary figures as David Sheppard. They preached the Word. He is concerned also to show how it works.